Original title:

Life Upgrade

Author: Clement Portlander

ISBN HARDBACK: 978-9916-88-312-9

ISBN PAPERBACK: 978-9916-88-313-6

The Road Less Traveled

In shadows deep, where few will tread,
A path unfolds, by whispers led.
With every step, the heart will brave,
Unknowns await, the bold and grave.

Footprints linger, tales untold,
In the silence, dreams unfold.
Embrace the bends, the twists of fate,
For in the wild, our spirits wait.

Rekindling the Flame

In ashes cold, a spark remains,
A flicker soft, against the chains.
With gentle breath, we stoke the light,
From weary dusk, ignites the night.

Memories dance in flickering glow,
The warmth returns, our hearts in tow.
Through whispered winds, we find our way,
Rekindled fire, our spirits sway.

Paving Fresh Paths

With hands outstretched, we carve the way,
New trails emerge, come what may.
Each step we take, a promise sworn,
In the soil of hope, new dreams are born.

The journey calls, both wide and vast,
A canvas fresh, our shadows cast.
Together we wander, side by side,
Through open fields, in joy we glide.

Awakening the Inner Phoenix

From ashes gray, we rise once more,
A vibrant flame, a heart to soar.
With wings outstretched, the heavens greet,
A dance of life, unbound, complete.

In trials faced, the strength emerges,
Through storms we fought, our spirit surges.
So let us fly, in colors bright,
Awakening dreams, to chase the light.

Gleaning Wisdom from Experience

Through trials faced and lessons learned,
We gather strength, in wisdom burned.
Each scar a story, each fall a chance,
To rise again, in life's vast dance.

The path is rough, the stones are hard,
Yet in the struggle, we find our guard.
With each misstep, our footing gains,
The seeds of insight sprout from pains.

The Symphony of New Choices

Every choice a note in time's grand score,
Each decision opens a brand-new door.
In harmony, we weave our fate,
With courage found, we dance, create.

A melody of paths entangle and sway,
Inviting us to play, to stray.
With every twist, a chance to sing,
In the symphony of life, we take wing.

Breaking Chains of Old

Chains that bind, once held so tight,
In clarity's glow, we find our light.
With strength anew, we shatter the past,
Embracing freedom, our shadows cast.

Each link of doubt, each fear unspun,
Transforms our hearts, ready to run.
With every step, we claim our might,
Breaking free into the night.

A Tapestry of New Dreams

Threads of hope in colors bright,
Weave together in the soft twilight.
From visions born in whispered sounds,
A tapestry of dreams astounds.

Each stitch a wish, each hue a song,
In this creation, we all belong.
With hearts aligned, we craft our way,
In this vibrant dance, we long to stay.

Fostering New Connections

In the heart where strangers meet,
New bonds are born, a dance so sweet.
Eyes connect, a silent spark,
Together lighting up the dark.

Laughter shared under the sky,
Moments captured, soaring high.
In whispers soft, the stories flow,
A tapestry of joy to grow.

Hands extend, a gracious touch,
In kindness found, we feel so much.
Building bridges, hearts laid bare,
Together weaving dreams we share.

As day turns bright, and nights unfold,
New paths before us start to mold.
With every step, a chance to see,
Connections grow, we're more than free.

Radiance Reimagined

Light refracts in colors bold,
Stories of the heart retold.
In silence whispers thoughts arise,
A world anew before our eyes.

Golden rays of warmth invoke,
The gentle laughter, words we spoke.
With shadows gone, we find our place,
In every smile, a soft embrace.

The dawn of dreams, the night of stars,
Together healing all our scars.
A vision bright, once dimmed by fears,
Now dances free through all the years.

With every heartbeat, we ignite,
The path of love, forever bright.
Each step we take to redefine,
Radiance flows, your hand in mine.

A Journey from Within

In quiet corners of the mind,
A treasure trove of thoughts we find.
Layers deep, the echoes call,
In stillness found, we learn to fall.

Wandering through the maze of dreams,
Life's whispers often teach in streams.
With every sigh, the truth unveils,
A compass forged, where heart prevails.

The winding road, both dark and light,
In searching soul, we find our sight.
Each twist and turn, a lesson clear,
To journey forth, we cast off fear.

With open hearts, we dare to seek,
The way to speak the words so meek.
In every heartbeat, wisdom's kin,
We find the love that starts within.

The Alchemy of Growth

In the soil of dreams, we sow our seeds,
With every storm, we face our needs.
Watered by hope, beneath the sun,
The journey starts when we first run.

Through trials and strife, we learn to bend,
In every challenge, we find a friend.
Roots reaching deep, a foundation laid,
With every step, we're unafraid.

Navigating Uncharted Waters

Sails set high, the winds do guide,
In open seas, our dreams collide.
Stars above like lanterns glow,
They show the path where courage goes.

With waves that crash, we stand our ground,
In every tempest, strength is found.
Hearts united, we steer our course,
Together we harness nature's force.

Blooms from Winter's End

From barren branches, life will spring,
Colorful petals, the earth will bring.
Awake from slumber, touch of sun,
Each bloom tells tales of battles won.

Whispers of warmth, in softest breeze,
Nature's canvas, we feel its ease.
Nature's promise, once hidden well,
Brings forth stories that flowers tell.

The Metamorphosis Within

In quiet spaces, change is born,
A spark ignites at break of dawn.
Cocooned in silence, seeds of thought,
In shadows cast, new forms are sought.

Emerging strong, like phoenix flame,
Transforming dreams, we shed our name.
Each layer shed, reveals the skin,
The journey starts with what's within.

The Mosaic of Becoming

Each piece a story untold,
Shadows dance, colors unfold.
Fragments brought near, they align,
Crafting a life, a design divine.

In the chaos, beauty grows,
Embracing change, as it flows.
From ashes rise, we learn to see,
Crafting our fate, set ourselves free.

Through trials faced, we're refined,
In struggles, our truths we'll find.
The paths we tread intertwine,
In each heartbeat, life's grand design.

With every choice, a shard we gain,
Together in joy, together in pain.
A mosaic bright, from dusk till dawn,
A journey of selves, forever drawn.

Finding the Light Within

In quiet corners, whispers call,
Echoes of hope where shadows fall.
Each breath a step toward the bright,
A flicker hidden, awaiting its flight.

Moments of silence, a sacred space,
Where we uncover our truest face.
From the depths, a fire ignites,
Guiding us through the longest nights.

In darkness, we learn to embrace,
The light that resides, our saving grace.
Hold it close, let courage unfurl,
For the light within can shift the world.

As we journey, hand in hand,
Illuminate paths across this land.
Together we shine, together we grow,
Finding the light in the love that we sow.

Beyond the Veil of Comfort

A cocoon of ease, it wraps so tight,
But outside lies the world, alive with light.
To break the shell and feel the breeze,
Is to dance with dreams and face the trees.

Fear whispers softly, a tale of woe,
Yet growth demands we dare to go.
Step into the unknown, embrace the fall,
For a heartbeat echoes the call of all.

With every leap, we shed the past,
In vulnerability, our spirits are cast.
Beyond comfort's veil, a new truth will thrive,
In the wildness of life, we come alive.

So take the hand of uncertainty near,
With courage kindled, dismissing fear.
Beyond the horizon, where wonders dwell,
We'll weave our tales, our hearts will swell.

The Horizon Beckons

Upon the edge where sky meets sea,
The horizon calls, a song of glee.
Whispers of journeys yet to unfold,
Tales of adventurers, brave and bold.

Colors mingle, a canvas in time,
Where dreams take flight, in prose and rhyme.
With each sunrise, new hopes ignite,
The horizon beckons, a dance of light.

Uncharted lands lie just ahead,
With each brave step, new paths are spread.
As the waves crash and the winds play,
Our spirits soar, come what may.

Together we'll wander, hand in hand,
Chasing the sun, traversing the sand.
For the horizon, it calls us near,
In the adventure of living, we have no fear.

Horizons of Hope

Beneath the rising sun's embrace,
Dreams awaken, find their place.
Gentle whispers in the air,
Promising a new affair.

Mountains high and valleys low,
Guide us where we long to go.
With every step, our hearts ignite,
Chasing shadows into light.

Tides of change will ebb and flow,
Yet still our spirits bravely show.
Together firm, we'll stand our ground,
In unity, our strength is found.

The Canvas of Tomorrow

Brush in hand, we start to dream,
Colors bright in radiant gleam.
Each stroke tells a tale untold,
A future bright, a vision bold.

Splashes of joy and hues of pain,
Life's masterpiece, we must maintain.
Mixing shades of hope and fears,
A tapestry woven through the years.

From darkness springs a vibrant glow,
Creating visions we can grow.
Together we'll paint the scenes,
Crafting life from vivid dreams.

Wings Unfurled

With every breath, we take to flight,
Soaring high, embracing light.
Wings unfurled, we chase the sky,
Leaving doubts that hold us shy.

The gusts of change, they lift us high,
Courage born, we spread and fly.
On currents of hope we glide,
Sharing dreams that swell inside.

No chains to bind, no fears to quell,
In freedom's arms, we dare to dwell.
Adventures near, horizons wide,
Together, let our spirits ride.

The Dance of Possibilities

In the twilight where dreams begin,
Possibilities spin and spin.
Every twirl a choice we make,
In this dance, we learn to wake.

Step by step, we find our way,
In the rhythm of the day.
With open hearts and minds so free,
We embrace what's yet to be.

Moments fleeting, yet they last,
In this dance, we break the past.
With each leap, we rise and shine,
Creating futures, yours and mine.

Renewal Pathways

In the stillness of dawn's light,
Whispers of change take flight.
Leaves unfurling from the ground,
Hope and promise all around.

Footsteps soft on winding trails,
Nature sings while sunlight pales.
Every step, a chance to grow,
In the heart, a gentle glow.

Rivers flow with stories told,
Carving paths through lands of gold.
Each moment a new embrace,
In this sacred, timeless space.

Renewal paints the world anew,
With every dawn, a vibrant hue.
Life flows in an endless song,
In these pathways, we belong.

The Horizon Beckons

Beneath the vast, unending sky,
The horizon calls, we must not shy.
Waves of color merge and blend,
A promise that journeys never end.

Footprints dance on sandy shores,
Echoes whisper of distant doors.
The sun dips low, a fiery glow,
With every breath, new dreams we sow.

Stars emerge as daylight wanes,
Charting paths on twilight's stains.
We chase the light, forever brave,
For in our hearts, the world we save.

The horizon beckons, clear and wide,
With open arms, we run, we glide.
Adventure waits, so draw your bow,
To new horizons, onward we go.

Blossoms in the Aftermath

In the wake of storms and strife,
Emerges beauty, sparking life.
Petals bloom where shadows cast,
Each flower whispers of the past.

Colors bright where gray once lay,
Nature's canvas, bold display.
Hope awakens, gently sings,
In the aftermath, renewal brings.

Roots embrace the earth so tight,
Holding fast through darkest night.
Blossoms rise from ground so deep,
Promises stirred from silent sleep.

Fragile threads of life perceive,
Patterns woven, we believe.
Through the ashes, grace will flow,
In each blossom, strength will grow.

Rising From Ashes

From the depths, we lift our gaze,
Emerging from the smoky haze.
With every breath, a new rebirth,
In the silence, find our worth.

Sparks ignite from flares of past,
Creating light that's made to last.
Wings unfurl where once was pain,
In rising hopes, we break the chain.

Each challenge faced becomes our root,
Nurturing strength, resolute.
In the fire's glow, we trust our way,
In the shadows, light will stay.

From the ashes, we arise,
With open hearts and clearer eyes.
In this journey, fierce and bold,
Rising from ashes, souls unfold.

Seeds of Change

In the earth, small seeds lie,
Whispers of hope, reaching high.
Every droplet sets them free,
From silent dreams, they long to be.

Roots will stretch and branches grow,
Transforming soil into glow.
Gentle winds will guide their way,
As they blossom, night to day.

Nature's canvas, brightly drawn,
With colors bright, a brand new dawn.
Every petal holds a tale,
In the garden, life prevails.

From tiny seeds, a world emerges,
With each heartbeat, the spirit surges.
Change begins in every heart,
As together, we'll take part.

A Kaleidoscope of Dreams

In the silence, dreams unfold,
Sparkling stories yet untold.
Colors swirl, they dance and play,
In this world where hopes can stay.

Through the lens of vibrant sights,
Imagination takes its flights.
Twisting visions, shaping fate,
In the dreams we cultivate.

Each reflection, a new design,
Mapping journeys, yours and mine.
Shifting patterns, endless views,
In our hearts, we dare to choose.

Step inside this wondrous sphere,
Where every dream is held so dear.
A kaleidoscope of pure delight,
Guiding us from dark to light.

Beyond the Comfort Zone

Step by step, we face the fear,
Beyond the walls that keep us near.
Testing waters, taking flight,
In the dark, there lies the light.

Stretching souls and breaking molds,
Finding strength in stories bold.
Every heartbeat, a chance to grow,
In the unknown, our spirits glow.

Risk the fall, embrace the climb,
In the challenge, we find our rhyme.
Wandering paths not seen before,
Beyond the comfort lies much more.

Together, let us find our way,
In the brave new world, we'll sway.
With open hearts, let's take the leap,
For dreams await in courage deep.

Embracing the New Dawn

As daylight breaks, the shadows fade,
Hope awakens, fears allayed.
In the morning, fresh and bright,
We embrace the power of light.

With open arms, the sun's embrace,
Guiding us to a sacred place.
Each moment holds a promise true,
In every breath, we start anew.

Let go of night, release the past,
For every moment cannot last.
In the dawn, our spirits rise,
Chasing visions through the skies.

Together, we will face the day,
Finding strength in every ray.
In this journey, hand in hand,
We'll write our dreams across the land.

Embracing the Unknown

In shadows deep, we step anew, A world uncharted waits
for you. With trembling hearts, we face the dark, Each
flicker holds a fragile spark.
The whispers soft, the signs unclear, Yet still we tread,
we cast off fear. For in the dark, a light may gleam, A
hidden truth, a distant dream.
We answer calls from voices strange, In foreign lands,
we feel the change. Each choice we make, each chance
we take, A woven path, a bond we stake.
Embrace the winds of fate's design, For in the unknown,
stars align. Each step a dance, each breath a song, The
journey's call will guide us along.

Blossoming Beyond Limits

In a garden where dreams take flight, Flowers bloom in pure delight. Each petal tells a story grand, Of hope and strength amidst the sand.
The roots stretch deep, the branches wide, We rise together, side by side. Through trials faced, our spirits soar, We reach for heights we've not explored.
The sun may set, yet dawn will break, In shadows cast, our hopes awake. With vibrant hues, we paint the air, A tapestry of love and care.
We learn to dance with life's embrace, Each moment lived, a sacred space. Beyond the limits, we shall thrive, In unity, we feel alive.

Echoes of Destiny

In echoes soft, our voices trace, The paths we've walked,
the time we face. Each memory a thread we've spun, In
tapestry, our lives are one.
The choices made, the dreams we weave, In every heart,
we dare believe. Through trials faced, we find our way,
The stars above show us to stay.
The laughter shared, the tears we've cried, In every
moment, hope resides. Each stepping stone, a mark of
grace, In destiny's dance, we find our place.
So hear the whispers of the past, In every heartbeat,
shadows cast. Our stories blend, a symphony, In echoes
of our destiny.

The Pathway to Renewal

Through tangled woods, we seek the light, A pathway
clear, yet out of sight. The journey long, the steps unsure,
Yet in our hearts, we feel the cure.
The leaves will turn, the seasons change, In every loss,
there's room for gain. With every dawn, new life will rise,
A time to dream, a chance to fly.
The river flows, it carves the stone, With patience
strong, we find our own. Each moment shared, a bloom
anew, The path ahead is bright and true.
So let us walk, hand in hand, Together strong, united
stand. For every step we dare to take, Leads to the joy
that we will make.

The Canvas of Tomorrow

On the horizon, colors blend,
Dreams await, around the bend.
Pencils poised, we sketch the time,
Each stroke whispers, hopes in rhyme.

A palette rich with light and shade,
Visions born, never to fade.
With every heartbeat, futures call,
A masterpiece awaits us all.

We paint with courage, not with fear,
Brush in hand, we hold it dear.
Each color tells a story true,
In the canvas, we find our hue.

Together, we will make it bright,
Illuminating darkest night.
In unity, our dreams will soar,
The canvas waits, let's create more.

Threads of Renewal

Through whispers of the ancient trees,
Life awakens in the gentle breeze.
Threads of gold in morning's glow,
Weaving tales of joy and woe.

Each stitch a promise, soft and strong,
Binding hearts where we belong.
In the fabric of our days,
Hope entwines in endless ways.

Seasons turn, an endless dance,
In each moment, find the chance.
To renew the spirit's song,
Threads of renewal keep us strong.

We'll mend the fabric, piece by piece,
In unity, our worries cease.
Together woven, we will stand,
In life's rich tapestry, hand in hand.

Breathing the Future

Inhale the dreams, exhale the doubt,
With every breath, we navigate the route.
Together we rise, hearts open wide,
In the flow of the future, we confide.

The air is thick with possibility,
In every pulse lies a new reality.
Exhale the past, breathe in the now,
With every moment, we make a vow.

Awake to the whispers of the dawn,
In the symphony of life, we're drawn.
With every heartbeat, we create,
Breathing the future, we cultivate.

Together we thrive, hearts aligned,
In every crease, wisdom we find.
Breathing in unity, hope, and light,
Towards a horizon, shining bright.

A Dance with Potential

Step by step, we learn to glide,
With every move, we feel the tide.
In rhythm with the universe, we sway,
Dancing with dreams that light the way.

The floor is set, and spirits rise,
Countless stars fill up the skies.
Each twirl a glimpse of what can be,
In this dance, we set our spirits free.

With every leap, we touch the air,
In the freedom found, we dare.
Potential flows in every spin,
A dance of life we find within.

Together we'll embrace the chance,
In perfect harmony, our souls dance.
With hearts aflame, and courage bold,
We twirl around, our stories told.

The Emergence of Radiance

In the dawn's gentle embrace,
Light unfurls with tender grace.
Shadows fade, fears take flight,
Hope ignites the heart's delight.

Whispers of dreams softly call,
Each moment cherished, big and small.
With every step, a spark we find,
A radiant path, beautifully designed.

Finding Joy in the Journey

Through winding roads where laughter plays,
We dance along the sunlit rays.
Each stumble met with a smile wide,
In the heart's rhythm, we confide.

Discovering treasures in each stride,
With friends and love, we take the ride.
In every challenge, joy we claim,
As life unfolds, we light the flame.

Tides of Transformation

Waves crash softly on the shore,
Whispers of change call for more.
As seasons shift, the seas may churn,
From each ebb, new lessons learn.

Miracles hide in the unknown,
In depths of courage, seeds are sown.
With heart and soul, we rise and flow,
Evolving with grace, like the tide's glow.

Breathing Life into Aspirations

With every breath, dreams take flight,
Inspiring hearts to chase the light.
A canvas waits for strokes so bold,
Within our hands, the future holds.

Kindled visions, bright and clear,
Shaping paths that draw us near.
With strength anew, we rise each day,
Breathing life into dreams, come what may.

Seeds of Tomorrow

In the soil, dreams reside,
Whispers of what's yet to be,
With each drop of rain, they guide,
Hope grows wild and free.

Nurtured by the sun's bright rays,
Life awakens from its sleep,
In the warmth of brighter days,
Promises in shadows deep.

Fingers crossed for what will sprout,
The future waits, a gentle call,
In every doubt, there lies a route,
Together, we can rise and fall.

With patience, we shall see them bloom,
From tiny seeds, a story spun,
A garden born to chase the gloom,
In unity, we'll find the sun.

Embracing the Unfamiliar

Step into the wild unknown,
Where shadows merge with light,
The heart sings a different tone,
As horizons take their flight.

Paths uncharted, dreams untold,
Adventures beckon, bright and vast,
In courage, find your heart of gold,
Embrace the present, leave the past.

A dance with fate, a twist of time,
Moments weave a tapestry,
In every challenge, find a rhyme,
Each new face, a mystery.

Together we shall laugh and cry,
In the arms of what we fear,
For in the strange, we learn to fly,
In the unfamiliar, we draw near.

A Journey in Full Bloom

From the seedling's quiet start,
To blossoms bursting forth with grace,
Each petal tells a tale of heart,
In every color, find your place.

With gentle rains and warming sun,
Life unfolds in vibrant hues,
A symphony for everyone,
In nature's hands, we find our muse.

Together, through the fields we roam,
Each step a verse in destiny,
Among the wildflowers, we find home,
In every breath, we feel so free.

So let the winds of change embrace,
Our stories woven with perfume,
A journey blooms, a sacred space,
In every heart, a garden's room.

Uncharted Territories

In lands where maps are yet to draw,
We step with wonder in our eyes,
Each mountain high, each river's flow,
A call to venture, seek the skies.

With every challenge, strength anew,
The footprints mark our paths of grace,
In quiet moments, visions brew,
Together, we will find our place.

Through forests thick and valleys wide,
The spirit of adventure calls,
In unity, we turn the tide,
No dream too big, no heart too small.

So here's to the tales we will weave,
In uncharted lands, we shall find,
The courage to dare, to believe,
In every corner, love so blind.

Breaking Free

From shadows deep, I find the light,
With wings unfurled, I take my flight.
No chains can bind my spirit's flame,
In the vast sky, I stake my claim.

The road ahead may twist and turn,
Through trials faced, I rise and learn.
Each step I take, a strength unveiled,
In the freedom sought, I shall not be jailed.

The past may whisper tales of pain,
But with each breath, I break the chain.
Embracing hope, I start anew,
With heart and courage, I will break through.

The world awaits, a canvas wide,
With every heartbeat, I decide.
For in my soul, the fire burns bright,
In breaking free, I reclaim my flight.

The Spark of Discovery

In quiet moments, thoughts take flight,
A single glimpse, ignites the night.
Curiosity whispers, soft and clear,
As paths unfold, new worlds appear.

Each question asked, a key in hand,
Unlocking doors to wonderland.
In every answer, mysteries lie,
The spark of truth, we must not shy.

Through trials faced, our minds expand,
With every venture, we take a stand.
Together we seek, a journey grand,
The spark of discovery, a guiding hand.

With every step, we learn to see,
The beauty found in curiosity.
In the quest for knowledge, we dive deep,
The spark of wonder, ours to keep.

Whispers of Potential

In the still of night, dreams start to weave,
A tapestry bright, of what we believe.
Whispers of change, soft as a breeze,
Call out our hearts, and urge us to seize.

The seeds we've sown, are waiting to bloom,
In the garden of life, dispelling the gloom.
Each moment embraced, a chance to grow,
Whispers of potential, in every shadow.

With courage ignited, we rise to the call,
To break through the silence, to stand tall.
For in every heartbeat, a purpose we find,
Whispers of potential, kind and unconfined.

Together we stand, in unity's grace,
As we chase our dreams, together we face.
The future awaits, a canvas to fill,
With whispers of potential, we conquer the hill.

Choreography of Change

In the dance of time, we sway and glide,
Through rhythms of life, we learn to bide.
Steps of uncertainty, we weave and spin,
In the choreography, our journey begins.

With each rotation, we let go of fear,
Embracing the moments, both far and near.
In every misstep, a lesson to glean,
The flow of change, a beautiful scene.

The stage is set, the lights aglow,
As we dance through trials, our spirits grow.
In harmony's song, we find our way,
In the choreography of change, we'll sway.

With every heartbeat, a rhythm unfolds,
In the dance of dreams, our stories told.
With grace, we move, side by side,
In this choreography, we take pride.

Chasing Brilliant Tomorrows

In the shimmer of the new day's light,
Hope unfurls its eager wings.
With dreams aloft, we take our flight,
And to the future, our spirit sings.

Each whisper of the morning breeze,
A promise held in heart and mind.
We dance through time with graceful ease,
Into the treasures we will find.

The path ahead, a canvas bright,
Where colors blend and visions flow.
With every step, we chase the light,
And let our vibrant hopes bestow.

Hand in hand, we greet the dawn,
With faith as strong as rivers grand.
Together, we will carry on,
To sculpt our dreams with steadfast hand.

The Dawn of Unwritten Chapters

Before us lies a world unknown,
Blank pages wait for tales to spill.
With ink of stars, our dreams are sown,
Each heartbeat amplifies the thrill.

In the silence, whispers call,
Of adventures yet to ignite.
We stand as one, we stand tall,
Embracing shadows, chasing light.

The clock ticks gently, time unfolds,
As stories weave through threads of fate.
With courage bold, we break the molds,
Our spirits soar, no room for hate.

New paths await, with twists and turns,
Together, let us dare to write.
With every step, a flame that burns,
In the dawn of chapters, pure delight.

Echoes in an Empty Hall

In the silence, whispers play,
Behind the doors that time forgot.
Memories linger, fade away,
In shadows where the light is caught.

Every step, a gentle sigh,
The walls recall a distant cheer.
A haunting tune that lifts on high,
Reminds us of the love held dear.

With echoes soft, the past unspools,
Reflecting joy and heartache, too.
In empty halls where silence rules,
We find the strength to push on through.

Though vacant space may seem so cold,
We gather warmth from what remains.
In echoes rich, our stories fold,
In every murmur, life sustains.

The Horizon's Embrace

As sunlight kisses ocean's edge,
The horizon blushes with the dawn.
In every wave, a whispered pledge,
To guide the dreams of those who yawn.

With open arms, the sky unfolds,
A tapestry of colors bright.
Each moment shared, a tale retold,
As day breaks gently into night.

Together we stand, hearts ablaze,
In the embrace of time's sweet flow.
Beyond the waves, we set our gaze,
For in the distance, wonders grow.

The horizon calls, a siren's song,
Promises linger in the air.
With every breath, we move along,
Into the future, brave and rare.

The Heart's Renaissance

In shadows deep, a spark resides,
Awakening love, where lost hope bides.
A symphony of whispers calls,
To rise again, as darkness falls.

With every breath, a promise made,
To heal the wounds, the heart has laid.
Embracing scars, with tender grace,
A journey blooms, in this sacred space.

Through trials faced, the spirit soars,
Rediscovering life behind closed doors.
A vibrant pulse, the anthem sings,
Of resilience born from broken strings.

In dawn's embrace, we find our way,
To cherish love that will not sway.
The heart's rebirth, a glorious art,
Eternal echo, a brand new start.

Tapestry of Transformation

Threads of silver, woven tight,
In the loom of day and night.
Each color tells a tale so bold,
Of change and growth, like stories told.

From shadows cast, a light ignites,
Transforming fears into guiding lights.
A dance unfolds, with every turn,
In the fire of dreams, we learn to burn.

The fabric stretches, yet never tears,
Embracing moments, hopes, and fears.
With every stitch, a world anew,
Creating beauty in all we do.

In the tapestry, we find our voice,
A symphony of hearts, we rejoice.
Together as one, we evolve and spin,
In this dance of life, we begin again.

Sunlit Steps Forward

With dawn's embrace, we rise and glow,
Step by step, through fields we go.
Chasing rays that warm the ground,
In every heartbeat, hope is found.

The path ahead, with shadows past,
Yet forward we tread, our spirits steadfast.
Each footfall echoes, a promise sweet,
In sunlit moments, our lives complete.

Together we walk, our laughter bright,
In the journey's embrace, we find our light.
Each step we take, a new refrain,
Building dreams amidst the rain.

In the golden hour, we share our dreams,
As sunlight dances on gentle streams.
With hearts aligned, we seek and soar,
In every step, we want for more.

Unfurling Hope's Petals

From silent buds, we stretch and bloom,
In the garden of dreams, dispelling gloom.
Each petal soft, a story untold,
Of resilience and strength, to uplift and hold.

With gentle winds, our colors rise,
Reaching for warmth in the vast, blue skies.
In the fragrance of life, we sway and dance,
Finding our voices in love's sweet chance.

As seasons change, we stand our ground,
In the heart of storms, we are bound.
Unfurling wide, our hopes take flight,
In the embrace of day and night.

For every petal that graces the air,
A reminder of life, and how we care.
In nature's grace, we find our way,
Unfurling hope, come what may.

Rising with the Dawn

Awake, the sun begins to rise,
Golden light in endless skies.
Birds are singing, a brand new day,
Chasing night, the shadows sway.

Softly whispers the morning breeze,
Rustling leaves on ancient trees.
Hope emerges, warm and bright,
Opening hearts to pure delight.

With every hue, the world's aglow,
Painting dreams in hues that flow.
Embrace this moment, fresh and new,
In the dawn, find strength anew.

Let the light guide every stride,
With the dawn, there's nothing to hide.
Together we rise, side by side,
In the beauty of morning's tide.

Transformations in the Mirror

Gazing deep into the glass,
Reflections shift as moments pass.
Stories etched upon each face,
Capturing time in silent grace.

Fractured images start to blend,
A symphony of lives transcend.
Each line tells of loss, of love,
Whispers echo from above.

Wounds that healed and scars that stay,
Painting paths of yesterday.
In this mirror, look and see,
The power of what used to be.

Embrace the changes, let them flow,
For in the depths, we learn and grow.
Transformations breathe through the night,
Guiding us toward the light.

Celestial Pathways of Change

Stars align in the night sky,
Guiding us as time goes by.
Constellations teach us flight,
Crafting dreams in cosmic light.

Each moment, a step we take,
Across the heavens, hearts awake.
In the silence, truths unfold,
Stories waiting to be told.

Galaxies swirl with vibrant hue,
Signaling paths that feel so true.
Through the dark, we find our way,
Celestial whispers lead the day.

Follow the light, let it inspire,
Sparks of change, ignite the fire.
Together we traverse the grand,
On celestial pathways, hand in hand.

The Art of Becoming

From shadows deep, a flicker glows,
With each step, the knowledge grows.
Crafting dreams with gentle hands,
Life's canvas stretches, expands.

Colors blend, emotions sway,
Expressing truths in every way.
With every brushstroke, we define,
The art of us, yours and mine.

Breaking chains that once confined,
In the chaos, peace we find.
Each tear shed, a lesson learned,
In the fire, resilience burned.

With open hearts, we learn to see,
The beauty in our journey, free.
In the making, we are strong,
The art of becoming is where we belong.

Shifting Sands of Existence

In a world where time wavers,
The dunes shift, tales unfold.
Each grain whispers a story,
Of lives, both young and old.

With each passing breeze of fate,
Dreams rise, then swiftly fall.
What once was firm beneath us,
Now drifts with the shifting call.

We stand at the edge of change,
Rooted in hope, yet unsure.
The horizon beckons brightly,
A promise, steady and pure.

Through layers of sand we search,
For truths that slip like the tide.
In this dance of existence,
We learn to trust, to abide.

The Ripple of Change

A stone cast into still waters,
Creates waves that touch the shore.
Each ripple tells of motion,
A soft pulse, forevermore.

In lives entwined with seasons,
We feel the tremors rise.
A whisper of the future,
Beneath the vast, starlit skies.

Moments echo into ages,
Transforming hearts and minds.
The ripple of our choices,
Leaves shadows that it finds.

Embrace the shifts around us,
Let currents guide your flow.
In the dance of life's water,
We find the strength to grow.

Bridges to New Realities

Between the worlds of now and then,
Bridges arch with hope and dreams.
Each step leads to unknown paths,
Where the light of wisdom beams.

Connections forged in heart and mind,
Cross rivers of doubt and fear.
Together, we build our future,
With love that draws us near.

Each plank a testament to trust,
Each nail a promise made.
In unity, we venture forth,
With courage unafraid.

Realities entwined in visions,
Create a tapestry bright.
We walk the bridges to tomorrow,
Guided by the stars' own light.

Flipping the Script

In a tale that's worn and tired,
We pause to turn the page.
With fresh ink, we rewrite fate,
Transforming fear to rage.

Characters that lost their way,
Find strength in new design.
Empowered by the changes,
They rise, embrace the shine.

Plot twists in life's narrative,
Bring laughter, tears, or grace.
As we learn to flip the script,
We reclaim our rightful place.

With every story rewritten,
Hope springs eternal anew.
In the theater of our lives,
We choose to play it true.

Unveiling Hidden Miracles

In the whisper of dawn's gentle light,
Unseen wonders take graceful flight.
Each breath a promise, each glance a gift,
In the stillness, our spirits drift.

Beneath the surface, secrets lie,
In the petals where dreams comply.
Hope lingers softly, like dew on grass,
In moments we cherish, they quietly amass.

The heart finds solace in what is near,
In silence, our visions become clear.
The bloom of joy in a hidden space,
A miracle found in a warm embrace.

So celebrate life's intricate art,
In every shadow, light plays its part.
Through the veil, let us boldly steer,
Unveiling miracles, year after year.

A Mosaic of Moments

Fragments of laughter, pieces of tears,
We weave together our hopes and fears.
Each moment a tile in a grand design,
A mosaic of memories, uniquely divine.

Sunset whispers, the moon takes its place,
In the dance of time, we find our grace.
Every heartbeat echoes, a subtle song,
In this tapestry woven, where we belong.

Fleeting glances, a touch of the hand,
In simple gestures, we make our stand.
Life's compass turns, guiding our way,
In the mosaic of moments, we brightly play.

So gather the pieces, let colors blend,
For in every finish, there lies a bend.
With each fragment cherished, our story flows,
A beautiful journey, as our spirit grows.

Futures Unwritten

A blank page lies before our eyes,
Where dreams can soar and passions rise.
The ink of hope flows freely here,
In futures unwritten, let's shed our fear.

Each step a promise, each choice a spark,
In the labyrinth of life, we embark.
Timeless horizons await our flight,
In the canvas of time, we ignite the night.

With every heartbeat, a chance to grow,
To chase the whispers the stars bestow.
The compass within guides us on our way,
Into the unknown, we dare to sway.

So let us write tales of laughter and love,
Embracing the journey as we rise above.
For futures unwritten are the paths we take,
In this wondrous adventure, our hearts awake.

Radiance in the Shadows

In the twilight where silence breathes,
A glow emerges, weaving through leaves.
Dancing softly, shadows play,
Radiance whispers, lighting the way.

Amid the night where doubts may creep,
A flicker of hope begins to leap.
Even in darkness, beauty persists,
In the hearts of those who dare to exist.

Stars sprinkle wisdom on the hidden ground,
In every silence, a strength is found.
With each heartbeat, the darkness fades,
As light finds a path where nothing evades.

So let us seek the glow within,
In every shadow, let courage begin.
For in the night, we claim our part,
Radiance shines from each hopeful heart.

Rewriting the Narrative

In shadows cast by doubt and fear,
Words like whispers vanish near.
With ink of courage, we will write,
A tale where hope ignites the light.

Pages turning, futures bright,
We seize the day, we claim our right.
A story bold, unique, and true,
Where every voice sings loud anew.

No more the tale of silent tears,
We paint the skies with dreams and cheers.
Unraveled knots from yesterday,
In freedom's dance, we'll find our way.

So, let us forge this path we've found,
On solid ground, our hearts unbound.
In every line, a chance to soar,
Our narrative, forevermore.

A Tapestry of Transformation

Threads of color, rich and bold,
Woven stories yet untold.
Each stitch a moment, all combined,
In this fabric, life defined.

Patterns shifting, shapes transform,
In the chaos, we find form.
Embracing change, we spin and weave,
A tapestry that helps us believe.

From frayed edges, we create,
A masterpiece that won't abate.
In hues of kindness, love, and grace,
We find our place, we find our space.

Let every fiber echo strong,
A chorus of where we all belong.
Together we will sew it tight,
A living art in day and night.

Awakening the Spark

In stillness found, a spark ignites,
A flicker dances, beckons flights.
With whispers soft, it calls our name,
To rise, to shine, to stake our claim.

The world awakens in the dawn,
New dreams arise, the past is gone.
With every heartbeat, passions swell,
Embrace the fire; it knows us well.

Beneath the surface, embers glow,
Hidden strength begins to flow.
Together, we fan the flames of fate,
United spirits, never late.

So let us dance in brilliant light,
Illuminate the endless night.
With every spark, we pave the way,
For brighter tomorrows, come what may.

The Journey of Rebirth

Through ashes cold, we rise anew,
A journey full of sights to view.
With every step, the past we shed,
A path of hope lies just ahead.

In whispered winds, a calling clear,
Embrace the change, relinquish fear.
With open hearts, we travel far,
Guided always by our star.

The river flows, our dreams take flight,
Beneath the moon, through darkest night.
With every challenge, strength is found,
In every heartbeat, love abounds.

So here we stand, reborn, alive,
In unity, we will thrive.
Our journey endless, ever bold,
In every chapter, life unfolds.

Resilient Threads

In the fabric of life, we weave our dreams,
Each thread a story, bursting at the seams.
Through storms and shadows, we hold on tight,
Resilient hearts shining, like stars in the night.

With every struggle, the colors blend,
Strength in the struggle, a beautiful trend.
We stitch our hopes in the tapestry bright,
Crafting a future, igniting the light.

Worn and frayed, yet never undone,
Every tear a lesson, every thread a run.
Bound by our journeys, we stand side by side,
Together we flourish, with love as our guide.

In the end, it's the love that we share,
The bonds that we nurture, a treasure so rare.
Threads may unravel, but hearts will mend,
In the rich tapestry, where all voices blend.

The Canvas of Intent

We paint our futures, brush in hand,
On the canvas of time, we make our stand.
Each stroke a choice, bold and sincere,
In the colors of passion, we banish fear.

With a palette of dreams, we blend and create,
A masterpiece waiting, it's never too late.
Daring to envision, we splash our hues,
A symphony vibrant, in reds, yellows, blues.

Mistakes are but shadows that shape our design,
Every flaw a detail, a moment divine.
We layer our visions, building them high,
With each stroke of purpose, we touch the sky.

As the canvas evolves, so do we all,
Embracing each color, we stand proud, we stand tall.
In the gallery of life, let's boldly present,
The beauty within us, the canvas of intent.

Carving Out Possibilities

With chisel in hand, we shape our own fates,
In the stone of existence, opportunity waits.
Each tap a decision, defining our path,
Crafting our future, escaping the wrath.

Every grain is a moment, a chance to explore,
We dig and we delve, discovering more.
In the echoes of passion, we hear the call,
The whispers of dreams that refuse to fall.

Through the dust and the rubble, we carve with care,
Finding the beauty hidden in layers so rare.
The sculptures of hope rise tall and proud,
In the gallery of life, we conquer the crowd.

As we chip away doubt, we summon our might,
Transforming the shadows into radiant light.
Every possibility waits in our hands,
A testament to courage, where a new world stands.

Chronicles of Change

In the pages of life, we write our tomorrows,
With ink made of dreams, and joy mixed with sorrows.
Each chapter a journey, each verse a new start,
We craft our own stories, with passion and heart.

As seasons keep turning, we learn and we grow,
The tales of our trials, like rivers, they flow.
Through moments of doubt, we gather our strength,
In the chronicles written, we find our own length.

Embracing the shifts, we welcome the change,
Each pivot a moment, sometimes feels strange.
But in the unpredictability, beauty will rise,
A testament to resilience, beneath the grey skies.

With every new sunrise, we turn the next page,
Collecting our wisdom, we step off the stage.
In the chronicles of time, our legacy remains,
A tapestry woven with love, joy, and pains.

Fresh Paint on Old Dreams

Brush strokes on canvas, colors collide,
Whispers of hope where memories hide.
A story reborn in hues so bright,
Old dreams refreshed, a brand new light.

Echoes of laughter still linger near,
With every stroke, I conquer my fear.
Chasing the visions that once slipped away,
Every false start leads to a new play.

A palette of wishes in shades of the past,
Reimagined futures, freedom at last.
The heart beats stronger, anew in its might,
Fresh paint on old dreams, igniting the night.

Colors blend boldly, no need for retreat,
In this vibrant dance, my soul feels complete.
Let the canvas capture what cannot be said,
With fresh paint on old dreams, I move ahead.

Metamorphosis of the Soul

In silence a whisper begins to grow,
A flicker of light in the shadows below.
The chrysalis waits, patient and still,
Yearning for daylight, embracing the thrill.

Wings unfold gently, vibrant and bold,
Shedding the past like a story retold.
Emerging from darkness, a radiant spark,
Dancing through life, leaving trails in the dark.

Transformation whispers with delicate grace,
Every moment cherished, a sacred space.
The journey untold, the spirit set free,
Metamorphosis sings its sweet melody.

From ashes of doubt, a new self will rise,
Wings catching the sun, reaching for skies.
With each breath I take, a promise unfolds,
Metamorphosis of the soul, timeless and bold.

Beyond Yesterday's Shadows

Footprints in sand fade with the tide,
Memories linger, yet no need to hide.
The sun breaks the dawn, a brand new day,
Beyond yesterday's shadows, I find my way.

Each step I take, a choice to believe,
In dreams that shimmer, I dare to achieve.
The past may shape me, but I hold the key,
Unlocking the future, setting me free.

Hope fills the air like a song on the breeze,
As I cast off the weight, I'm learning to seize.
With courage as armor, I rise and ignite,
Beyond yesterday's shadows, I dance in the light.

A canvas of moments, a tapestry spun,
Threads of my journey, woven as one.
No longer a prisoner of what's gone before,
Beyond yesterday's shadows, I'm ready for more.

Climbing New Heights

The mountain looms high, a challenge ahead,
With every footstep, old fears are shed.
Clouds may obscure the path to my goal,
Yet deep in my heart, I feel the climb's toll.

Each rock that I grasp is a lesson in strength,
With each breath I take, I measure the length.
Violent winds howl, but they won't steal my dreams,
For climbing new heights, I follow the streams.

The summit calls softly, an inviting song,
With courage and faith, I know I belong.
In moments of doubt, I remember the fire,
The passion inside fuels my deepest desire.

Upward I rise, though the journey is steep,
The promise of vistas inspires my leap.
With every ascent, a piece of me grows,
Climbing new heights, embracing what flows.

Wings Unfurled

In the dawn's gentle light,
A bird takes to the sky,
With feathers full of dreams,
It soars, bold and high.

The world below it calls,
Paths yet to be trod,
With each powerful beat,
It dances with God.

Through storms and through skies,
No fear of the fall,
For freedom is found,
When we answer the call.

With wings outspread wide,
We embrace the unknown,
Like the bird in the air,
We are never alone.

The Alchemy of Growth

In the quiet of the night,
Seeds whisper their dreams,
Buried deep in the soil,
They reach for sunbeams.

Time is a gentle hand,
Nurturing each sprout,
With patience as its art,
Transforming doubt.

Leaves unfurl like hope,
Colors vibrant and bright,
From darkness to full bloom,
They dance in the light.

Growth is a journey,
Crafted through the years,
Turning pain into strength,
Transforming our fears.

Navigating New Waters

A ship upon the waves,
With sails full and white,
Challenges lie ahead,
Yet the heart holds tight.

Storms may rage and roar,
The compass may sway,
But the soul knows its course,
Through dark and through gray.

With each wave that crashes,
Lessons will unfold,
In depths of the ocean,
New stories are told.

Together we'll steer,
In this vast, boundless sea,
For every new horizon,
Calls out brave and free.

The Chisel and the Clay

In a sculptor's strong hands,
The cold clay does lie,
With vision and with love,
Transformations arise.

Chipping away the doubts,
Each strike reveals form,
Through patience and through time,
From chaos emerges norm.

The chisel sings a song,
Of beauty and of grace,
Molding simple clay,
Into a timeless face.

Art is born of struggle,
With each gentle caress,
Creating from the heart,
In imperfection, bless.

Shifting Sands of Existence

In the desert of time, we wander alone,
Chasing shadows that whisper of home.
Each grain holds a story, of loss and of gain,
Carried by winds, like a soft, whispered pain.

Footprints fade swiftly, yet memories last,
Each step writes a tale that is shaped by the past.
We dance on this canvas, of shifting and change,
Seeking the solace in moments so strange.

The sun rises slowly, a fire in the sky,
Painting the horizon, as day passes by.
The sands shift beneath us, in rhythm with breath,
Reminding us daily of life intertwined with death.

In a world ever-changing, we stand and we sway,
Embracing the ebb of the night into day.
With every horizon, a promise we find,
In the shifting of sands, our souls are aligned.

The Quest for Renewal

In the heart of the forest, where silence resides,
Awakens the spirit, where hope never hides.
Leaves fresh and green, in the soft morning light,
Whispers of promise take flight with the night.

With each gentle raindrop, the earth holds its breath,
Rebirth in the shadows, defying all death.
Every flower that blooms, is a story retold,
Of dreams lost and found, of the brave and the bold.

Climbing the mountains, the view is anew,
Each challenge embraced, like a dawn breaking through.
The quest for renewal, a journey divine,
To rise from the ashes, in hopes we align.

In the arms of the wild, we surrender our fears,
Renewed by the passage of countless years.
A tapestry woven, with threads of the past,
In the quest for renewal, our spirits hold fast.

Awakening the Spirit

A hush falls around, as the day starts to wake,
Gentle whispers of life, in the stillness they break.
The sun, a soft promise, begins to ignite,
Awakening spirits, chasing shadows from night.

In the dance of the leaves, the breezes take flight,
Nature's symphony plays in the heart of the light.
Each note of the morning is pure and divine,
An orchestra rising, a spirit entwined.

In the glow of the dawn, our hearts start to leap,
Reclaiming the dreams that we buried so deep.
With every deep breath, our souls start to soar,
Awakening the spirit, who craved to explore.

In the laughter of children, in the rustle of trees,
The spirit awakens, to dance with the breeze.
This miracle of moments, together we share,
Awakening the spirit, our burdens laid bare.

A Symphony of New Beginnings

In the hush of the twilight, a new song ignites,
A symphony rising, to dance with the nights.
Each note like a heartbeat, a promise reborn,
In the melody of life, new horizons adorn.

With each gentle whisper, the dawn breaks anew,
Painting the skies in vibrant hues.
The music of tomorrow, begins with a dream,
A symphony echoing, in soft, flowing streams.

Faced with the challenge, we rise and embrace,
The rhythm of change, each step we retrace.
Notes intertwining, like lives in the song,
In the grand orchestration, we all belong.

Let the chords of compassion and hope fill the air,
A symphony playing, to remind us to care.
With each rising verse, let our spirits unite,
In the symphony of new beginnings, we find our light.

New Beginnings Unfold

In dawn's soft light, we stand anew, A canvas fresh, a
path in view. The whispers of hope fill the air, With
every heartbeat, dreams lay bare.

The past, a tale, now set aside, With open arms, we take
the stride. Embracing change, we shed the old, A story
bright, waiting to be told.

Beneath the stars, our spirits rise, Each moment
cherished, no goodbyes. The future calls, a sweet
embrace, In every heartbeat, find your place.

New beginnings bloom, like flowers bold, In every heart,
a journey unfolds. With courage strong, we spread our
wings, To dance with joy, as life now sings.

The Art of Reinvention

With every breath, we find our way, The stories twist, the colors play. In silence deep, we seek the end, For every curve, we twist and bend.

From ashes cold, we rise again, A phoenix bright, we seek the zen. With courage fierce, we shed the fear, In each new shape, the path is clear.

The mirror shows a face renewed, In every glance, our hearts imbued. With every turn, we break the mold, A canvas wide, our truth unfolds.

In reinvention, life takes flight, We find our song in darkest night. The art of change, a wondrous dance, With open hearts, we take the chance.

A Symphony of Changes

In every note, a story lies, A symphony beneath the skies.
The rhythms shift, the tempo flows, A dance of life,
where beauty grows.

From silence deep, the music swells, In vibrant tones,
each spirit tells. The echoes ring of joy and pain, A
tapestry of love's sweet gain.

As seasons shift, we learn to sway, The notes of life, our
grand ballet. In harmony, we find our grace, Each
heartbeat a song, our sacred space.

A symphony of changes bright, In every turn, we find the
light. With every heartbeat, melodies blend, A journey
grand, where dreams transcend.

Echoes of Tomorrow

In twilight's glow, the shadows play, Echoes whisper of
another day. Tomorrow's dreams, a canvas wide, In
every heart, our hopes reside.

From yesterdays, we learn and grow, The seeds of change
begin to show. In every moment, futures spark, A
guiding light within the dark.

The winds of time, they softly call, With courage strong,
we rise, we fall. In echoes sweet, our hopes are cast, A
journey shared, a love that lasts.

Tomorrow waits, beyond the bend, Each step we take,
new worlds extend. With hearts unbound, we chase the
dawn, In echoes bright, our dreams are drawn.

Horizons of Hope

Beyond the mountains, skies unfold,
A whisper of dreams, stories untold.
Each dawn arises, bright and clear,
With every heartbeat, we draw near.

Beneath the stars, our wishes soar,
In the distance, we seek the shore.
The waves of time wash over sand,
Together we stand, hand in hand.

Through storms we journey, winds may howl,
Yet in the dark, our spirits growl.
With hope as our guide, we'll navigate,
In every struggle, we'll cultivate.

So let the horizon stretch and gleam,
We'll chase the light, fulfill the dream.
With courage ignited, hearts so wide,
We find our way, with hope as our guide.

The Garden of Renewal

In the quiet earth, seeds lie in wait,
For gentle hands to nurture fate.
With sunlit days and moonlit nights,
Life awakens, in vibrant sights.

The blossoms bloom, colors ignite,
Filling the air with pure delight.
Each petal tells a tale of grace,
In nature's arms, we find our place.

The rain will fall, the winds will sweep,
Yet in this garden, dreams we'll keep.
With every season, lessons grow,
In this sacred space, we learn to flow.

So tend the flowers, hear their song,
In the garden of life, we all belong.
With love as our soil, we'll rise anew,
A testament to all we can do.

Echoes of Ambition

With whispers loud, ambition calls,
Each echo bounces off the walls.
In every heartbeat, dreams ignite,
A fire within, a guiding light.

Through shadowed paths, we carve our fate,
Against the odds, we won't abate.
The heights we seek may seem afar,
Yet in our souls, we know we are.

We gather strength with every fall,
Embracing failures, standing tall.
For in the struggle, growth we find,
A journey crafted, heart and mind.

So let the echoes lead the way,
In every challenge, we will stay.
With passion's fire, we'll rise and soar,
Chasing the dreams that we adore.

From Ashes to Ascension

From the ashes, hope will rise,
A phoenix born beneath the skies.
Through trials faced, the spirit mends,
In every heart, the light transcends.

The flames of sorrow may burn deep,
Yet from the darkness, we won't sleep.
With every tear, we find our strength,
In unity, we'll go to length.

The journey's hard, the road is long,
But from our struggles, we grow strong.
With wings spread wide, we'll learn to fly,
Embracing life as we touch the sky.

Together we'll rise, with love adorned,
From ashes to heights, we feel reborn.
In every heartbeat, new paths unfurl,
Ascension found in this beautiful world.

Milton Keynes UK
Ingram Content Group UK Ltd.
UKHW020936041024
449263UK00011B/555